Clear Sky, Pure Light

ENCOUNTERS WITH
HENRY DAVID THOREAU

Clear Sky, Pure Light

Compiled & Edited by
CHRISTOPHER CHILDS

with an Introduction by
WALTER HARDING

and Wood Engravings by
MICHAEL McCURDY

THE PENMAEN PRESS LIMITED
Lincoln, Massachusetts

First Edition

Acknowledgements

FOR ASSISTANCE in selecting and editing the material for *Clear Sky, Pure Light*, I am deeply grateful to Anne McGrath of the Thoreau Lyceum; I am also indebted to Walter Harding and Milton Meltzer, co-authors of *A Thoreau Profile*, and especially to Charles R. Anderson, editor of *Thoreau's World: Miniatures From His Journal*: in those volumes I first made the acquaintance of a number of the following passages. My sincere thanks also to John Briggs, for criticizing both the Foreword and the commentaries; and to all the many, many other people who have contributed to both this project and its theatrical sibling.

Grateful acknowledgement is made to the New York University Press, for permission to quote material from *The Correspondence of Henry David Thoreau* (ed. by Walter Harding and Carl Bode; N.Y.U. Press, 1958); and to the firm of Brandt and Brandt, for permission to quote briefly from the essay, 'The American Loneliness,' by the late Thornton Wilder, originally published in the *Atlantic Monthly* of August, 1952.

In the production of the stage portrait, as in many other projects, I was the recipient of the support, encouragement, and generous patronage of Mary C. Newbold. That she could not live to see this volume in print touches the event of its publication with sadness.

For Hugh Fortmiller and David Gardner
who first illustrated to me
the true dignity and value of the theatre,
and for Anne McGrath & Heddie Kent
who still illustrate to me
the virtues of Concord.

Contents

Selections from different sources (or from different or non-sequential sections of the same source) are separated by the ornament ❧. Selections separated by only a line space are from the same source, with some material omitted.

Introduction

WHAT IS THERE about Henry David Thoreau that so intrigues and compels us? He himself says in *Walden*, 'How many a man has dated a new era in his life from the reading of a book.' And *Walden* has been that book for so many of us. It has changed the whole pattern of people's lives. I know whereof I speak, for the whole pattern of my own life has been changed by the reading of *Walden*. It has led me for more than forty years now to devoting the greater part of my life, vocationally and avocationally, to trying to understand its author more fully. Why? Not only because he has come to represent for me man, but also because I find with each new day that my search for him gives new meaning, new understanding to my own life. As the late president of the Thoreau Society, Ted Bailey, once said, 'I shall never be rid of Henry.' And neither will I. I am Thoreau driven. (It would not be inappropriate at this time to quote Thoreau once more: 'I should not talk so much about myself if there were anybody else whom I knew as well'!)

Christopher Childs, too, is, I believe, Thoreau driven. As is so obvious in his 'Foreword'—and in his life—*Walden* and Henry Thoreau have come into his life and have become an integral part of that life. He has become a true Thoreauvian, not in that he has become more like Thoreau, but in that he has become more of himself. That is the sign of the true Thoreauvian. ('I would not have any one adopt *my* mode of living,' says Thoreau, 'on any account; for, beside that before he has fairly learned it I may have found out another for myself, I desire that there may be as many different persons in the world as possible; but I would have each one be very careful to find out and pursue *his own* way, and not his father's or his mother's or his neighbor's instead.')

There have been many attempts to recreate Henry Thoreau in poetry and fiction and drama. One of my own first projects on Thoreau nearly forty years ago was to compile a 'Bibliography of Thoreau in Poetry, Fiction and Drama' (*Bulletin of Bibliography*, May, 1943) and it listed more than a hundred such attempts. (If that list were to be brought up-to-date, it would be three or four times that long, for the attempts have proliferated.). But one of the disenchanting results of my study was the realization of how few of those poets, playwrights, and novelists caught the true spirit of the man they were trying to depict. They

sentimentalized him or made him cute or made him ob-
noxious. The Thoreau they created usually turned out not
to be *the* Thoreau, but *their* Thoreau.

It was thus with some trepidation that three years ago
on a visit to Concord I walked one evening into the community playhouse on Walden Street to first see Christopher Childs perform his *Clear Sky, Pure Light*. Although I
knew somewhat of his project—I had corresponded with
him and talked occasionally on the phone when he was re-
searching the background for his play so that I knew his
intent was great, and although several friends of mine
whose opinions on Thoreau I respected highly, enthusias-
tically endorsed it, I entered the theatre with some misgivings and even an admixture of hostility—I did not want
to endure someone else's misconceptions of Thoreau; I
wanted to see the true Thoreau or none at all. But I must
confess that my misgivings and hostility lasted at the most
ten minutes once the curtain was up and the performance
had begun, for here through the genius of Christopher
Childs I was seeing the erinaceous, the gentle; the pro-
found, the lighthearted; the joyous, the thoughtful Thoreau
I had come to know after years of search. This was not
Christopher Childs' Thoreau; it was *the* Thoreau.

Many years ago my old friend Leonard Gray wrote a
little plea against all the -ists and -isms trying to take over
Henry Thoreau to prove that he was a communist or an

anti-communist, a pacifist or a war-monger, a nudist or a puritan, or whatever. Gray entitled his little plea 'Let Thoreau Be Thoreau.' Christopher Childs has not tried to make Thoreau over into any preconceived image. He has presented him honestly and faithfully as he was. He has 'let Thoreau be Thoreau.' That was the charm of the dramatization of *Clear Sky, Pure Light*. And that charm has carried over to this book version too. Read it and meet Henry Thoreau just as pertinent and impertinent, to use one of his own favorite puns, as he was in real life.

WALTER HARDING
State University of New York
at Geneseo
April 5, 1978

Foreword

I AM by profession an actor. I reside, however — by choice or by chance; I have never been able to decide which — primarily outside the mainstream of the American theatre. In a tributary, perhaps, but one I seem to have largely to myself. There are few other vessels in sight, though occasionally and delightfully one comes within hailing distance and we converse across the water about the wind, the weather or the tides.

Quite probably my situation would be analagous no matter what my profession; I was a teacher before I was an actor, and isolated from the majority of my colleagues then as now. This volume marks the renewal of an old acquaintance with the literary professions, but I expect that no matter how deep my involvement with the world of letters may ever become, I will obstinately, irascibly and resolutely maintain a position in the periphery. Generally speaking, I like it out here. I can see better and breathe a little more freely.

Clear Sky, Pure Light

The material between these covers is the material from which, in 1974, I first began to draw a 'stage portrait' of Henry David Thoreau, eventually enabling myself to make a living in the theatre independent of producers, booking agents and even other actors. The choice and arrangement of the selections that follow, and the nature of the brief commentary between them, imply an interpretation of Thoreau's character; out in the periphery, arrogantly situated, I stand cheerfully by it. Part of my justification for this impertinent stance is suggested by the statements above: even offstage, in my daily life, I maintain a strong sense of identification with various aspects of Thoreau's personality. (This is sometimes counterproductive. For example, I have just noticed that at least three images in the preceding paragraphs are unconsciously 'borrowed' from Thoreau. Well. A reader or two may be challenged to identify them.)

However, the real point of this book is not to attempt a definitive portrait of Henry Thoreau. At this late date, we are all pretty much free to make of him what we will, for better or worse—those whose critical and sympathetic faculties are both richly developed will surely understand him best. I write these words a few short miles from Walden Pond, now a landmark for the world, and the point of this book is something any actor (which, Shakespeare notes, really should mean anyone) will understand: legendary though he has become, Thoreau was not an abstraction; he was a living, sentient man, with or through whom we can all identify ourselves. And, in that sense, he—like John Brown—is not gone. He treads the streets of Concord; scouts the ridges of Katahdin and Monadnock; overlooks the sea at Staten Island; and he walks the shores of Walden with each of us.

CHRISTOPHER CHILDS
Wyndstowe Farm, Stow, Massachusetts
24 February 1978

The stage version of Clear Sky, Pure Light, *subtitled* an Evening with Henry David Thoreau, *opened on* July 6, 1975, *at Concord's Bicentennial Memorial Center. It has subsequently been toured regionally and nationally to schools, colleges and other sponsoring institutions.*

A PREFACE:
SPEECH AND SILENCE

A few yards from the site of Thoreau's Walden cabin rises the skeleton of a lone, giant pine, perhaps the last still standing of a generation planted in the previous century; close by rests one of its fallen contemporaries. Their presence is soundless eloquence . . . the perfect counterpoint to the words their near predecessors helped inspire.

A related contrast, the awareness of which preoccupied Thoreau in some of his earliest writing, is the subject of these opening selections. The first, spoken by candlelight, serves as a Prologue to the theatrical version of this 'portrait'; both serve to introduce ideas that go near the core of Thoreau's philosophy.

AS THE TRUEST SOCIETY approaches always nearer to solitude, so the most excellent speech finally falls into Silence. Silence is audible to all men, at all times, and in all places. She is when we hear inwardly, sound when we hear outwardly. Creation has not displaced her, but is her visible framework and foil. All sounds are her servants and purveyors, proclaiming not only that their mistress is, but is a rare mistress, and earnestly to be sought after. They are so far akin to Silence, that they are but bubbles on her surface, which straightway burst, an evidence of the strength and prolificness of the under-current; a faint utterance of silence, and then only agreeable to our auditory nerves when they contrast themselves with and relieve the former. In proportion as they do this, and are heighteners and intensifiers of the Silence, they are harmony and purest melody.

Silence is the universal refuge, the sequel to all dull discourses and all foolish acts, a balm to our every chagrin, as welcome after satiety as after disappointment; that background which the painter may not daub, be he master or bungler, and which, however awkward a figure we may have made in the foreground, remains ever our inviolable asylum, where no indignity can assail, no personality disturb us.

IT WERE in vain for me to endeavor to interpret the Silence. She cannot be done into English. For six thousand years men have translated her with what fidelity belonged to each, and still she is little better than a sealed book. A man may run on confidently for a time, thinking he has her under his thumb, and shall one day exhaust her, but he too must at last be silent, and men remark only how brave a beginning he made; for when he at length dives into her, so vast is the disproportion of the told to the untold, that the former will seem but the bubble on the surface where he disappeared. Nevertheless, we will go on, like those Chinese cliff swallows, feathering our nests with the froth which may one day be bread of life to such as dwell by the seashore.

❧

DO NOT SPEAK for other men; speak for yourself.

THOUGH you should only speak to one kindred mind in all time, though you should not speak to one, but only utter aloud, that you may the more completely realize and live in the idea which contains the reason for your life, that you may build yourself up to the height of your conceptions, that you may remember your Creator in the days of your youth and justify His ways to man, that the end of life may not be its amusement, speak—though your thought presupposes the non-existence of your hearers— thoughts that transcend life and death.

RIVER:
WILDNESS AND CIVILIZATION

✣

In an age when unlimited mobility on land seems almost the norm, we tend to forget one of the chief avenues of Thoreau's day: the River, now perceived by the majority as a primarily local and recreational resource.

But the Concord, winding quietly on, still leads to the Merrimac; and the Merrimac, east to the sea, and north to the mountains. Follow Thoreau, briefly, as he describes setting out ('we two, brothers, and natives of Concord, weighed anchor in this river port') on the 1839 journey he would later immortalize in his Week on the Concord and Merrimack Rivers; *take Concord as a real or symbolic point of departure, as you choose. The territory entered is not exclusively geographical.*

I HAVE NEVER GOT over my surprise that I should have been born into the most estimable place in the world, and in the very nick of time, too.

⚜

I THINK I could write a poem to be called 'Concord.' For argument I should have the River, the Woods, the Ponds, the Hills, the Fields, the Swamps and Meadows, the Streets and Buildings, and the Villagers.

⚜

CONCORD RIVER is remarkable for the gentleness of its current, which is scarcely perceptible, and some have referred to its influence the proverbial moderation of the inhabitants of Concord, as exhibited in the Revolution, and on later occasions.

⚜

WITH such thoughts we swept gently by this now peaceful pasture ground, on waves of Concord, in which was long since drowned the din of war.

[9]

Clear Sky, Pure Light

❧

GRADUALLY the village murmur subsided, and we seemed to be embarked on the placid current of our dreams, floating from past to future as silently as one awakes to fresh morning or evening thoughts.

❧

BY NOON we were let down into the Merrimack through the locks at Middlesex, just above Pawtucket Falls, by a serene and liberal-minded man, who came quietly from his book, though his duties, we supposed, did not require him to open the locks on Sundays.

❧

WE WERE THUS ENTERING the State of New Hampshire on the bosom of the flood formed by the tribute of its innumerable valleys. The river was the only key which could unlock its maze, presenting its hills and valleys, its lakes and streams, in their natural order and position.

I HAVE TRACED its stream from where it bubbles out of the rocks of the White Mountains above the clouds, to where it is lost amid the salt billows of the ocean on Plum Island beach. At first it comes on murmuring to itself by the base of stately and retired mountains, through moist primitive woods whose juices it receives, where the bear still drinks it, and the cabins of settlers are far between, and there are few to cross its stream; enjoying in solitude its cascades still unknown to fame; by long ranges of mountains of Sandwich and of Squam, slumbering like tumuli of Titans, with the peaks of Moosehillock, the Haystack, and Kearsarge reflected in its waters; where the maple and the raspberry, those lovers of the hills, flourish amid temperate dews; — flowing long and full of meaning, but untranslatable as its name Pemigewasset, by many a pastured Pelion and Ossa, where unnamed muses haunt, tended by Oreads, Dryads, Naiads, and receiving the tribute of many an untasted Hippocrene. There are earth, air, fire, and water, — very well, this is water, and down it comes.

> Such water do the gods distil,
> And pour down every hill
>   For their New England men;
> A draught of this wild nectar bring,
> And I'll not taste the spring
>   Of Helicon again.

Falling all the way, and yet not discouraged by the lowest fall. By the law of its birth never to become stagnant, for it has come out of the clouds, and down the sides of precipices worn in the flood, through beaver dams broke loose, not splitting but splicing and mending itself, until it found a breathing place in this low land. There is no danger now that the sun will steal it back to heaven again before it reach the sea, for it has a warrant even to recover its own dews into its bosom again with interest at every eve.

ISSUING FROM the iron region of Franconia, and flowing through still uncut forests, by inexhaustible ledges of granite, with Squam, and Winnepisiogee, and Newfound, and Massabesic lakes for its millponds, it falls over a succession of natural dams, where it has been offering its *privileges* in vain for ages, until at last the Yankee race came to *improve* them.

❦

SOME SPRING the white man came, built him a house, and made a clearing here, letting in the sun, dried up a farm, piled up the old gray stones in fences, cut down the pines around his dwelling, planted orchard seeds brought from the old country, and persuaded the civil apple tree to blossom next to the wild pine and the juniper, shedding its perfume in the wilderness. Their old stocks still remain. He culled the graceful elm from out the woods and from the river-side, and so refined and smoothed his village plot. And thus he plants a town.

THE WHITE MAN comes, pale as the dawn, with a load of thought, with a slumbering intelligence as a fire raked up, knowing well what he knows, not guessing but calculating;

strong in community, yielding obedience to authority; of experienced race; of wonderful, wonderful common sense; dull but capable, slow but persevering, severe but just, of little humor but genuine; a laboring man, despising game and sport; building a house that endures, a framed house. He buys the Indian's moccasins and baskets, then buys his hunting grounds, and at length forgets where he is buried, and plows up his bones.

❧

WE TALK of civilizing the Indian, but that is not the name for his improvement. By the wary independence and aloofness of his dim forest life he preserves his intercourse with his native gods, and is admitted from time to time to a rare and peculiar society with Nature. He has glances of starry recognition to which our saloons are strangers. The steady illumination of his genius, dim only because distant, is like the faint but satisfying light of the stars compared with the dazzling but ineffectual and short-lived blaze of candles.

THE INDIAN'S INTERCOURSE with Nature is at least such as admits of the greatest independence of each. If he is somewhat of a stranger in her midst, the gardener is too much of a familiar.

IF WE COULD LISTEN but for an instant to the chaunt of the Indian muse, we should understand why he will not exchange his savageness for civilization. Nations are not whimsical. Steel and blankets are strong temptations; but the Indian does well to continue Indian.

❧

I AM CONVINCED that my genius dates from an older era than the agricultural. I would at least strike my spade into the earth with such careless freedom but accuracy as the woodpecker his bill into a tree. There is in my nature, methinks, a singular yearning toward all wildness. I know of no redeeming qualities in myself but a sincere love for some things, and when I am reproved I fall back on to this ground. What have I to do with plows? I cut another furrow than you see. Where the off ox treads, there is it not, it is further off; where the nigh ox walks, it will not be, it is nigher still. If corn fails, my crop fails not, and what are drought and rain to me?

❧

HEAL YOURSELVES, doctors; by God I live.

GODS

❧

Crystallized dogma is not the stuff of which true religion is made: religion is based on mystery. Those strong enough to stand away from dogma perceive the extent to which it can limit its adherents. A few are also irritable enough to speak out against it, and they keep alive religions worthy of our respect.

IT SEEMS to me that the god that is commonly worshipped in civilized countries is not at all divine, though he bears a divine name, but is the overwhelming authority and respectability of mankind combined. Men reverence one another, not yet God. If I thought that I could speak with discrimination and impartiality of the nations of Christendom, I should praise them, but it tasks me too much. They seem to be the most civil and humane, but I may be mistaken. Every people have gods to suit their circumstances; the Society Islanders had a god called Toahitu, 'in shape like a dog; he saved such as were in danger of falling from rocks and trees.' I think that we can do without him, as we have not much climbing to do. Among them a man could make himself a god out of a piece of wood in a few minutes, which would frighten him out of his wits.

THERE ARE various, nay incredible faiths; why should we be alarmed at any of them? What man believes, God believes.

Clear Sky, Pure Light

I TRUST that some may be as near and dear to Buddha or Christ, or Swedenborg, who are without the pale of their churches. It is necessary not to be Christian, to appreciate the beauty and significance of the life of Christ. I know that some will have hard thoughts of me, when they hear their Christ named beside my Buddha, yet I am sure that I am willing they should love their Christ more than my Buddha, for the love is the main thing, and I like him too. Why need Christians be still intolerant and superstitious?

MOST PEOPLE with whom I talk, men and women even of some originality and genius, have their scheme of the universe all cut and dried, — very *dry*, I assure you, to hear, dry enough to burn, dry-rotted and powder-post, me-thinks, — which they set up between you and them in the shortest intercourse; an ancient and tottering frame with all its boards blown off. They do not walk without their bed. Some to me seemingly very unimportant and unsubstantial things and relations, are for them everlastingly settled, — as Father, Son, and Holy Ghost, and the like. These are like the everlasting hills to them. But in all my wanderings, I never came across the least vestige of authority for these things. They have not left so distinct a trace as the delicate flower of a remote geological period on the coal in my grate. The wisest man preaches no doctrines; he has no scheme; he sees no rafter, not even a cobweb, against the heavens. It is clear sky. If I ever see more clearly at one time than at another, the medium through which I see is clearer. To see from earth to heaven, and see there standing, still a fixture, that old Jewish scheme! What right have you to hold up this obstacle to my understanding you, to your understanding me! You did not invent it; it was imposed on you. Examine your authority.

YOUR SCHEME must be the framework of the universe; all other schemes will soon be ruins. The perfect God in his revelations of himself has never got to the length of one such proposition as you, his prophets, state. Have you learned the alphabet of heaven, and can count three? Do you know the number of God's family? Can you put mysteries into words? Do you presume to fable of the ineffable? Pray, what geographer are you, that speak of heaven's topography? Whose friend are you that speak of God's personality? Do you, Miles Howard, think that he has made you his confidant? Tell me of the height of the mountains of the moon, or of the diameter of space, and I may believe you, but of the secret history of the Almighty, and I shall pronounce thee mad. Yet we have a sort of family history of our God, — so have the Tahitians of theirs, — and some old poet's grand imagination is imposed on us as adamantine everlasting truth, and God's own word!

ON BEING A WRITER

Humorists are not alone in their possession of a sense of humor, and if Thoreau showed little inclination to compete in literary matters with the likes of Twain or Dickens, he was nevertheless no stranger to the comic or ironic insight. He also had the ability to see his own efforts in a humorous perspective. A few readers, unaware of this, may be surprised by the following passage.

FOR A YEAR or two past, my *publisher*, falsely so called, has
been writing from time to time to ask what disposition
should be made of the copies of 'A Week on the Concord
and Merrimack Rivers' still on hand, and at last suggesting
that he had use for the room they occupied in his cellar. So
I had them all sent to me here, and they have arrived to-day
by express, filling the man's wagon — 706 copies out of an
edition of 1000 which I bought of Munroe four years ago and
have been ever since paying for, and have not quite paid
for yet. The wares are sent to me at last, and I have an opportunity to examine my purchase. They are something
more substantial than fame, as my back knows, which has
borne them up two flights of stairs to a place similar to that
to which they trace their origin. Of the remaining two hundred and ninety and odd, seventy-five were given away,
the rest sold. I have now a library of nearly nine hundred
volumes, over seven hundred of which I wrote myself. Is it
not well that the author should behold the fruits of his

labor? My works are piled up on one side of my chamber half as high as my head, my *opera omnia*. This is authorship; these are the work of my brain. There was just one piece of good luck in the venture. The unbound were tied up by the printer four years ago in stout paper wrappers, and inscribed, —

H. D. Thoreau's

Concord River

50 cops.

So Munroe had only to cross out 'River' and write 'Mass.' and deliver them to the expressman at once. I can see now what I write for, the result of my labors.

Nevertheless, in spite of this result, sitting beside the inert mass of my works, I take up my pen to-night to record what thought or experience I may have had, with as much satisfaction as ever. Indeed, I believe that this result is more inspiring and better for me than if a thousand had bought my wares. It affects my privacy less and leaves me freer.

LOSS

❧

John Thoreau, Jr., with whom Henry had journeyed on the Concord and Merrimac, died of lockjaw, at the age of twenty-seven, on the twelfth of January, 1842. Waldo Emerson, eldest child of Lidian and Ralph Waldo, and Thoreau's favorite in the family — with whom he had been living — died on the twenty-fourth of that same month, nine months short of his sixth birthday.

At least part of the reason Thoreau felt the need to retire to Walden, 'drive life into a corner' and consider 'whether it is of the devil or of God' is suggested by these excerpts from two letters written in the following March.

THE SUN has just burst through the fog, and I hear blue-birds, song-sparrows, larks, and robins down in the mead-ow. The other day I walked in the woods, but found my-self rather denaturalized by late habits. Yet it is the same nature that Burns and Wordsworth loved the same life that Shakspeare and Milton lived. The wind still roars in the wood, as if nothing had happened out of the course of nature. The sound of the waterfall is not interrupted more than if a feather had fallen.

Nature is not ruffled by the rudest blast—The hurri-cane only snaps a few twigs in some nook of the forest. The snow attains its average depth each winter, and the chic-adee lisps the same notes. The old laws prevail in spite of pestilence and famine. No genius or virtue so rare & revo-lutionary appears in town or village, that the pine ceases to exude resin in the wood, or beast or bird lays aside its habits.

How plain that death is only the phenomenon of the individual or class. Nature does not recognize it, she finds her own again under new forms without loss. Yet death is beautiful when seen to be a law, and not an accident—It is as common as life. Men die in Tartary, in Ethiopia—in England—in Wisconsin. And after all what portion of this so serene and living nature can be said to be alive? Do this year's grasses and foliage outnumber all the past.

Every blade in the field—every leaf in the forest—lays down its life in its season as beautifully as it was taken up. It is the pastime of a full quarter of the year. Dead trees—sere leaves—dried grass and herbs—are not these a good part of our life? And what is that pride of our autumnal scenery but the hectic flush—the sallow and cadaverous countenance of vegetation—its painted throes—with the November air for canvas—

When we look over the fields are we not saddened because the particular flowers or grasses will wither—for the law of their death is the law of new life. Will not the land be in good heart *because* the crops die down from year to year? The herbage cheerfully consents to bloom, and wither, and give place to a new.

So it is with the human plant. We are partial and selfish when we lament the death of the individual, unless our plaint be a paean to the departed soul, and a sigh as the wind sighs over the fields, which no shrub interprets into its private grief.

One might as well go into mourning for every sere leaf

—but the more innocent and wiser soul will snuff a fragrance in the gales of autumn, and congratulate Nature upon her health.

After I have imagined thus much will not the Gods feel under obligation to make me realize something as good.

❧

ONLY NATURE has a right to grieve perpetually, for she only is innocent.

I DO NOT WISH to see John ever again—I mean him who is dead—but that other whom only he would have wished to see, or to be, of whom he was the imperfect representative. For we are not what we are, nor do we treat or esteem each other for such, but for what we are capable of being.

As for Waldo, he died as the mist rises from the brook, which the sun will soon dart his rays through. Do not the flowers die every autumn? He had not even taken root here. I was not startled to hear that he was dead;—it seemed the most natural event that could happen. His fine organization demanded it, and nature gently yielded its request. It would have been strange if he had lived. Neither will nature manifest any sorrow at his death, but soon the note of the lark will be heard down in the meadow, and fresh dandelions will spring from the old stocks where he plucked them last summer. I have been living ill of late, but am now doing better.

ON IMPROVEMENTS

❧

There is a general (and fortunate) agreement that a man has some degree of control over his own destiny. Thoreau regarded the degree of control as relative to the amount of determination and practical wisdom in the individual. Hence his disdain for the multitude who accepted 'quiet desperation' as their lot.

I WOULD FAIN SAY something, not so much concern-
ing the Chinese and Sandwich Islanders as you who read
these pages, who are said to live in New England; something about your condition, especially your outward condition or circumstances in this world, in this town, what it
is, whether it is necessary that it be as bad as it is, whether
it cannot be improved as well as not. I have travelled a
good deal in Concord; and everywhere, in shops, and of-
fices, and fields, the inhabitants have appeared to me to be
doing penance in a thousand remarkable ways. What I have
heard of Bramins sitting exposed to four fires and looking
in the face of the sun; or hanging suspended, with their
heads downward, over flames; or looking at the heavens
over their shoulders 'until it becomes impossible for them
to resume their natural position, while from the twist of the
neck nothing but liquids can pass into the stomach;' or
dwelling, chained for life, at the foot of a tree; or measuring
with their bodies, like caterpillars, the breadth of vast

empires; or standing on one leg on the tops of pillars,— even these forms of conscious penance are hardly more incredible and astonishing than the scenes which I daily witness. The twelve labors of Hercules were trifling in comparison with those which my neighbors have undertaken; for they were only twelve, and had an end; but I could never see that these men slew or captured any monster or finished any labor.

I SOMETIMES WONDER that we can be so frivolous, I may almost say, as to attend to the gross but somewhat foreign form of servitude called Negro Slavery, there are so many keen and subtle masters that enslave both North and South. It is hard to have a Southern overseer; it is worse to have a Northern one; but worst of all when you are the slave-driver of yourself.

PUBLIC OPINION is a weak tyrant compared with our own private opinion. What a man thinks of himself, that it is which determines, or rather indicates, his fate.

THE MASS OF MEN lead lives of quiet desperation. What is called resignation is confirmed desperation. From the desperate city you go into the desperate country, and have to console yourself with the bravery of minks and muskrats. A stereotyped but unconscious despair is concealed even under what are called the games and amusements of mankind. There is no play in them, for this comes after work. But it is a characteristic of wisdom not to do desperate things.

When we consider what, to use the words of the catechism, is the chief end of man, and what are the true necessaries and means of life, it appears as if men had deliberately chosen the common mode of living because they preferred it to any other. Yet they honestly think there is no choice left. But alert and healthy natures remember that the sun rose clear. It is never too late to give up our prejudices. No way of thinking or doing, however ancient, can be trusted without proof. What everybody echoes or in silence passes by as true to-day may turn out to be falsehood to-morrow, mere smoke of opinion, which some had trusted for a cloud that would sprinkle fertilizing rain on their fields.

THE WOODS, AND WALDEN

❧

Thoreau's relationship with the natural world was astonishingly personal without being sentimental. It was certainly not that he projected human qualities onto the face of nature; rather, one feels, he sensed in himself those qualities most present in his natural surroundings. But that is only a part of the story.

FOR A LONG TIME I was reporter to a journal, of no very wide circulation, whose editor has never yet seen fit to print the bulk of my contributions, and, as is too common with writers, I got only my labor for my pains. However, in this case my pains were their own reward.

For many years I was self-appointed inspector of snow-storms and rain-storms, and did my duty faithfully; surveyor, if not of highways, then of forest paths and all across-lot routes, keeping them open, and ravines bridged and passable at all seasons, where the public heel had testified to their utility.

I have looked after the wild stock of the town, which give a faithful herdsman a good deal of trouble by leaping fences; and I have had an eye to the unfrequented nooks and corners of the farm; though I did not always know whether Jonas or Solomon worked in a particular field to-day; that was none of my business. I have watered the red huckleberry, the sand cherry and the nettle tree, the red pine and the black ash, the white grape and the yellow violet, which might have withered else in dry seasons.

In short, I went on thus for a long time (I may say it without boasting), faithfully minding my own business, till it became more and more evident that my townsmen would not after all admit me into the list of town officers, nor make my place a sinecure with a moderate allowance. My accounts, which I can swear to have kept faithfully, I have, indeed, never got audited, still less accepted, still less paid and settled. However, I have not set my heart on that.

FINDING THAT my fellow-citizens were not likely to offer me any room in the court house, or any curacy or living anywhere else, but I must shift for myself, I turned my face more exclusively to the woods, where I was better known. I determined to go into business at once, and not wait to acquire the usual capital, using such slender means as I had already got. My purpose in going to Walden Pond was not to live cheaply nor to live dearly there, but to transact some private business with the fewest obstacles; to be hindered from accomplishing which for want of a little common sense, a little enterprise and business talent, appeared not so sad as foolish.

I HAVE THOUGHT that Walden Pond would be a good place for business, not solely on account of the railroad and the ice trade; it offers advantages which it may not be good policy to divulge; it is a good port and a good foundation.

❧

NEVERTHELESS, of all the characters I have known, perhaps Walden wears best, and best preserves its purity. Many men have been likened to it, but few deserve that honor. Though the woodchoppers have laid bare first this shore and then that, and the Irish have built their sties by it, and the railroad has infringed on its border, and the ice-men have skimmed it once, it is itself unchanged, the same water which my youthful eyes fell on; all the change is in me. It has not acquired one permanent wrinkle after all its ripples. It is perennially young, and I may stand and see a swallow dip apparently to pick an insect from its surface as of yore. It struck me again to-night, as if I had not seen it almost daily for more than twenty years,—Why, here is Walden, the same woodland lake that I discovered so many years ago; where a forest was cut down last winter another is springing up by its shore as lustily as ever; the same thought is welling up to its surface that was then; it is the same liquid joy and happiness to itself and its Maker, ay, and it *may* be to me. It is the work of a brave man surely, in whom there was no guile! He rounded this water with his hand, deepened and clarified it in his thought, and in his will bequeathed it to Concord. I see by its face that it is visited by the same reflection; and I can almost say, Walden, is it you?

RESISTANCE TO
CIVIL GOVERNMENT

The following essay is reasonably well known. It is articulate, it is forceful, and, despite its references to a particular period of a particular national history, its theme shows every sign of being timeless and universal.

For all that, it is a deeply personal statement by a man who had an abiding conviction that right and wrong are separable entities. If its message is universal, its style is unmistakably individual. Nothing could possibly be more appropriate.

I HEARTILY ACCEPT the motto, — 'That government is best which governs least;' and I should like to see it acted up to more rapidly and systematically. Carried out, it finally amounts to this, which also I believe, — 'That government is best which governs not at all;' and when men are prepared for it, that will be the kind of government which they will have.

THIS AMERICAN GOVERNMENT, — what is it but a tradition, though a recent one, endeavoring to transmit itself unimpaired to posterity, but each instant losing some of its integrity? It has not the vitality and force of a single living man; for a single man can bend it to his will.

BUT IT IS NOT the less necessary for this; for the people must have some complicated machinery or other, and hear its din, to satisfy that idea of government which they have. Governments show thus how successfully men can be imposed on, even impose on themselves, for their own advantage. It is excellent, we must all allow; yet this government never of itself furthered any enterprise, but by the alacrity with which it got out of its way. *It* does not keep the country free. *It* does not settle the West. *It* does not educate. The character inherent in the American people has done all that has been accomplished; and it would have done somewhat more, if the government had not sometimes got in its way. For government is an expedient by which men would fain succeed in letting one another alone; and, as has been said, when it is most expedient, the governed are most let alone by it.

But, to speak practically and as a citizen, unlike those who call themselves no-government men, I ask for, not at once no government, but *at once* a better government. Let every man make known what kind of government would command his respect, and that will be one step toward obtaining it.

After all, the practical reason why, when the power is once in the hands of the people, a majority are permitted, and for a long period continue, to rule, is not because they are most likely to be in the right, nor because this seems fairest to the minority, but because they are physically the strongest. But a government in which the majority rule in all cases cannot be based on justice, even as far as men understand it. Can there not be a government in which majorities do not virtually decide right and wrong, but conscience?—in which majorities decide only those questions to which the rule of expediency is applicable? Must the citizen ever for a moment, or in the least degree, resign his conscience to the legislator? Why has every man a conscience, then? I think that we should be men first, and subjects afterward. It is not desirable to cultivate a respect for the law, so much as for the right. The only obligation which I have a right to assume, is to do at any time what I think right. It is truly enough said, that a corporation has no conscience; but a corporation of conscientious men is a corporation *with* a conscience. Law never made men a whit more just; and, by means of their respect for it, even the well-disposed are daily made the agents of injustice. A common and natural result of an undue respect for law is, that you may see a file of soldiers, colonel, captain, corporal, privates, powder-monkeys and all, marching in admirable order over hill and dale to the wars, against their wills, aye, against their common sense and consciences, which makes it very steep marching indeed, and produces a palpitation of the heart. They have no doubt that it is a damnable business in which they are concerned; they are all peaceably inclined. Now, what are they? Men at all? or small moveable forts and magazines, at the service of some unscrupulous man in power?

[*47*]

Clear Sky, Pure Light

THE MASS OF MEN serve the State thus, not as men mainly, but as machines, with their bodies.

A VERY FEW, as heroes, patriots, martyrs, reformers in the great sense, and *men*, serve the State with their consciences also, and so necessarily resist it for the most part; and they are commonly treated by it as enemies.

HOW DOES it become a man to behave toward this American government to-day? I answer that he cannot without disgrace be associated with it. I cannot for an instant recognize that political organization as *my* government which is the *slave's* government also.

All men recognize the right of revolution; that is, the right to refuse allegiance to and to resist the government, when its tyranny or its inefficiency are great and unendurable. But almost all say that such is not the case now. But such was the case, they think, in the Revolution of '75. If one were to tell me that this was a bad government because it taxed certain foreign commodities brought to its ports, it is most probable that I should not make an ado about it, for I can do without them: all machines have their friction; and possibly this does enough good to counterbalance the evil. At any rate, it is a great evil to make a stir about it. But when the friction comes to have its machine, and oppression and robbery are organized, I say, let us not have such a machine any longer. In other words, when a sixth of the population of a nation which has undertaken to be the refuge of liberty are slaves, and a whole country is unjustly overrun and conquered by a foreign army, and subjected to military law, I think that it is not too soon for honest men to rebel and revolutionize. What makes this duty the more urgent is the fact, that the country so over-run is not our own, but ours is the invading army.

THIS PEOPLE must cease to hold slaves, and to make war on Mexico, though it cost them their existence as a people.

I HAVE PAID no poll-tax for six years. I was put into a jail once on this account, for one night; and, as I stood con-sidering the walls of solid stone, two or three feet thick, the door of wood and iron, a foot thick, and the iron grating which strained the light, I could not help being struck with the foolishness of that institution which treated me as if I were mere flesh and blood and bones, to be locked up. I wondered that it should have concluded at length that this was the best use it could put me to, and had never thought to avail itself of my services in some way. I saw that, if there was a wall of stone between me and my towns-men, there was a still more difficult one to climb or break through, before they could get to be as free as I was. I did not for a moment feel confined, and the walls seemed a great waste of stone and mortar. I felt as if I alone of all my townsmen had paid my tax. They plainly did not know how to treat me, but behaved like persons who are under-bred. In every threat and in every compliment there was a blunder; for they thought that my chief desire was to stand the other side of that stone wall. I could not but smile to see how industriously they locked the door on my meditations, which followed them out again without let or hindrance, and *they* were really all that was dangerous. As they could not reach me, they had resolved to punish my body; just as boys, if they cannot come at some person against whom they have a spite, will abuse his dog. I saw that the State was half-witted, that it was timid as a lone woman with her silver spoons, and that it did not know its friends from its foes, and I lost all my remaining respect for it, and pitied it.

Thus the State never intentionally confronts a man's sense, intellectual or moral, but only his body, his senses. It is not armed with superior wit or honesty, but with superior physical strength. I was not born to be forced. I will breathe after my own fashion. Let us see who is the strongest. What force has a multitude? They only can force me who obey a higher law than I. They force me to become like themselves. I do not hear of *men* being *forced* to live this way or that by masses of men. What sort of life were that to live? When I meet a government which says to me, 'Your money or your life,' why should I be in haste to give it my money? It may be in a great strait, and not know what to do: I cannot help that. It must help itself: do as I do. It is not worth the while to snivel about it. I am not responsible for the successful working of the machinery of society. I am not the son of the engineer. I perceive that, when an acorn and a chestnut fall side by side, the one does not remain inert to make way for the other, but both obey their own laws, and spring and grow and flourish as best they can, till one, perchance, overshadows and destroys the other. If a plant cannot live according to its nature, it dies; and so a man.

RETURN

Few of us manage to exercise our freedom of thought and action to the extent that Thoreau did. For that reason we are inclined to envy his foray to Walden, romanticize it, and often neglect the fact that his stay at the pond represented only one period of Thoreau's life—and a relatively brief one at that. Metaphorically speaking, Thoreau built many cabins by many Waldens.

Biologists and anthropologists are quick to note that one of the human species' strong points is adaptability. We seem, however, to regard the idea somewhat wistfully, and without great confidence that it applies specifically to each of us. Thoreau clearly asserts that it does.

WHEN I WROTE the following pages, or rather the bulk of them, I lived alone, in the woods, a mile from any neighbor, in a house which I had built myself, on the shore of Walden Pond, in Concord, Massachusetts, and earned my living by the labor of my hands only. I lived there two years and two months. At present I am a sojourner in civilized life again.

❧

BUT WHY I changed? why I left the woods? I do not think that I can tell. I have often wished myself back. I do not know any better how I ever came to go there. Perhaps it is none of my business, even if it is yours. Perhaps I wanted a change. There was a little stagnation, it may be. About 2 o'clock in the afternoon the world's axle creaked as if it needed greasing, as if the oxen labored with the wain and could hardly get their load over the ridge of the day. Perhaps if I lived there much longer, I might live there forever. One would think twice before he accepted heaven on such terms. A ticket to Heaven must include tickets to Limbo, Purgatory, and Hell. Your ticket to the boxes admits you to the pit also.

❧

I LEFT the woods for as good a reason as I went there. Perhaps it seemed to me that I had several more lives to live, and could not spare any more time for that one. It is remarkable how easily and insensibly we fall into a particular route, and make a beaten track for ourselves. I had not lived there a week before my feet wore a path from my door to the pond-side; and though it is five or six years since I trod it, it is still quite distinct. It is true, I fear, that others may have fallen into it, and so helped to keep it open. The surface of the earth is soft and impressible by the feet of men; and so with the paths which the mind travels. How worn and dusty, then, must be the highways of the world, how deep the ruts of tradition and conformity! I did not wish to take a cabin passage, but rather to go before the mast and on the deck of the world, for there I could best see the moonlight amid the mountains. I do not wish to go below now.

❧

I MUST SAY that I do not know what made me leave the pond. I left it as unaccountably as I went to it. To speak sincerely, I went there because I had got ready to go; I left it for the same reason.

Return

꙰

I LEARNED this, at least, by my experiment: that if one advances confidently in the direction of his dreams, and endeavors to live the life which he has imagined, he will meet with a success unexpected in common hours. He will put some things behind, will pass an invisible boundary; new, universal, and more liberal laws will begin to establish themselves around and within him; or the old laws be expanded, and interpreted in his favor in a more liberal sense, and he will live with the license of a higher order of beings. In proportion as he simplifies his life, the laws of the universe will appear less complex, and solitude will not be solitude, nor poverty poverty, nor weakness weakness. If you have built castles in the air, your work need not be lost; that is where they should be. Now put the foundations under them.

ON THE NATURE AND ORIGIN
OF AN ACCIDENT

✣

We like to simplify our great men, to purify them of paradoxes, to gloss over or forget the ironies and inconsistencies that marked their lives. But, as to err is only human, even great men have lesser moments. Part of the fascination they eventually hold for us lies in the way they react to their own foibles and follies.

I ONCE SET FIRE to the woods. Having set out, one April day, to go to the sources of Concord River in a boat with a single companion, meaning to camp on the bank at night or seek a lodging in some neighboring country inn or farmhouse, we took fishing tackle with us that we might fitly procure our food from the stream, Indian-like. At the shoemaker's near the river, we obtained a match, which we had forgotten. Though it was thus early in the spring, the river was low, for there had not been much rain, and we succeeded in catching a mess of fish sufficient for our dinner before we had left the town, and by the shores of Fair Haven Pond we proceeded to cook them. The earth was uncommonly dry, and our fire, kindled far from the woods in a sunny recess in the hillside on the east of the pond, suddenly caught the dry grass of the previous year which grew about the stump on which it was kindled. We sprang to extinguish it at first with our hands and feet, and then we fought it with a board obtained from the boat, but in a few minutes it was beyond our reach; being on the side of a hill, it spread rapidly upward, through the long, dry, wiry grass interspersed with bushes.

'Well, where will this end?' asked my companion. I saw that it might be bounded by Well Meadow Brook on one side, but would, perchance, go to the village side of the brook. 'It will go to town,' I answered. While my companion took the boat back down the river, I set out through the woods to inform the owners and to raise the town. The fire had already spread a dozen rods on every side and went leaping and crackling wildly and irreclaimably toward the wood. That way went the flames with wild delight, and we felt that we had no control over the demonic creature to which we had given birth. We had kindled many fires in the woods before, burning a clear space in the grass, without ever kindling such a fire as this.

As I ran toward the town through the woods, I could see the smoke over the woods behind me marking the spot and progress of the flames. The first farmer whom I met driving a team, after leaving the woods, inquired the cause of the smoke. I told him. 'Well,' said he, 'it is none of my stuff,' and drove along. The next I met was the owner in his field, with whom I returned at once to the woods, running all the way. I had already run two miles. When at length we got into the neighborhood of the flames, we met a carpenter who had been hewing timber, an infirm man who had been driven off by the fire, fleeing with his axe. The farmer returned to hasten more assistance. I, who was spent with running, remained. What could I do alone against a front of flame half a mile wide?

I walked slowly through the wood to Fair Haven Cliff, climbed to the highest rock, and sat down upon it to observe the progress of the flames, which were rapidly approaching me, now about a mile distant from the spot where the fire was kindled. Presently I heard the sound of the distant bell giving the alarm, and I knew that the town was on its way to the scene. Hitherto I had felt like a guilty person, — nothing but shame and regret. But now I settled the matter with myself shortly. I said to myself: 'Who are these men who are said to be the owners of these woods, and how am I related to them? I have set fire to the forest, but I have done no wrong therein, and now it is as if the lightning had done it. These flames are but consuming their natural food.' (It has never troubled me from that day to this more than if the lightning had done it. The trivial fishing was all that disturbed me and disturbs me still.) So shortly I settled it with myself and stood to watch the approaching flames. It was a glorious spectacle, and I was the only one there to enjoy it. The fire now reached the base of the cliff and then rushed up its sides. The squirrels ran before it in blind haste, and three pigeons dashed into the midst of the smoke. The flames flashed up the pines to their tops, as if they were powder.

When I found I was about to be surrounded by the fire, I retreated and joined the forces now arriving from the town. It took us several hours to surround the flames with our hoes and shovels and by back fires subdue them. In the midst of all I saw the farmer whom I first met, who had turned indifferently away saying it was none of his stuff, striving earnestly to save his corded wood, his stuff, which the fire had already seized and which it after all consumed.

It burned over a hundred acres or more and destroyed much young wood. When I returned home late in the day, with others of my townsmen, I could not help noticing that the crowd who were so ready to condemn the individual who had kindled the fire did not sympathize with the owners of the wood, but were in fact highly elate and as it were thankful for the opportunity which had afforded them so much sport; and it was only half a dozen owners, so called, though not all of them, who looked sour or grieved, and I felt that I had a deeper interest in the woods, knew them better and should feel their loss more, than any or all of them. The farmer whom I had first conducted to the woods was obliged to ask me the shortest way back, through his own lot. Why, then, should the half dozen owners [and] the individuals who set the fire alone feel sorrow for the loss of the wood, while the rest of the town have their spirits raised? Some of the owners, however, bore their loss like men, but other some declared behind my back that I was a 'damned rascal;' and a flibbertigibbet or two, who crowed like the old cock, shouted some reminiscences of 'burnt woods' from safe recesses for some years after. I have had nothing to say to any of them.

FRIENDSHIP
AND
SINGULARITY

Thornton Wilder maintained that the distance Thoreau sensed between himself and those around him 'was aggravated by the vastness of his expectations.' Wilder went on to comment that this insistent demand for perfection is an obstacle deeply and broadly present in the American character. That may serve to explain why Thoreau's thoughts on friendship and solitude have long struck a resonant, yet often melancholy, chord in many of his readers.

I KNOW OF but one or two persons with whom I can afford to walk. With most the walk degenerates into a mere vigorous use of your legs, ludicrously purposeless, while you are discussing some mighty argument, each one having his say, spoiling each other's day, worrying one another with conversation, hustling one another with our conversation. I know of no use in the walking part in this case, except that we may seem to be getting on together toward some goal; but of course we keep our original distance all the way. Jumping every wall and ditch with vigor in the vain hope of shaking your companion off. Trying to kill two birds with one stone, though they sit at opposite points of compass, to see nature and do the honors to one who does not.

⚘

WE HAVE such a habit of looking away that we see not what is around us. How few are aware that in winter, when the earth is covered with snow and ice, the phenomenon of the sunset sky is double! The one is on the earth around us, the other in the horizon. These snow-clad hills answer to the rosy isles in the west.

THUS THE SKY and the earth sympathize, and are subject to the same laws, and in the horizon they, as it were, meet and are seen to be one.

I have walked in such a place and found it hard as marble.

꙰

EVERYWHERE SNOW, gathered into sloping drifts about the walls and fences, and, beneath the snow, the frozen ground, and men are compelled to deposit the summer's provision in burrows in the earth like the ground squirrel. Many creatures, daunted by the prospect, migrated in the fall, but man remains and walks over the frozen snow-crust and over the stiffened rivers and ponds, and draws now upon his summer stores. Life is reduced to its lowest terms. There is no home for you now, in this freezing wind, but in that shelter which you prepared in the summer. You steer straight across the fields to that in season. I can with difficulty tell when I am over the river. There is a similar crust over my heart. Where I rambled in the summer and gathered flowers and rested on the grass by the brook-side in the shade, now no grass nor flowers, no brook nor shade, but cold, unvaried snow, stretching mile after mile, and no place to sit.

Friendship and Singularity

٭

I KNEW a crazy man who walked into an empty pulpit one Sunday and, taking up a hymn-book, remarked: 'We have had a good fall for getting in corn and potatoes. Let us sing Winter.' So I say, 'Let us sing winter.' What else can we sing, and our voices be in harmony with the season?

٭

HERE I AM at home. In the bare and bleached crust of the earth I recognize my friend.

٭

HOW LONG we will follow an illusion! On meeting that one whom I call my friend, I find that I had imagined something that was not there. I am sure to depart sadder than I came. Nothing makes me so dejected as to have met my friends, for they make me doubt if it is possible to have any friends. I feel what a fool I am. I cannot conceive of persons more strange to me than they actually are; not thinking, not believing, not doing as I do; interrupted by me. My only distinction must be that I am the greatest bore they ever had. Not in a single thought agreed; regularly balking one another. But when I get far away, my thoughts return to them. That is the way I can visit them. Perhaps it is unaccountable to me why I care for them. Thus I am taught that my friend is not an actual person. When I have withdrawn and am alone, I forget the actual person and remember only my ideal. Then I have a friend again. I am not so ready to perceive the illusion that is in Nature. I certainly come nearer, to say the least, to an actual and joyful intercourse with her. Every day I have more or less communion with her, as I think. At least, I do not feel as if I must withdraw out of nature. I feel like a welcome guest. Yet, strictly speaking, the same must be true of nature and of man; our ideal is the only real.

❦

I LONG for wildness, a nature which I cannot put my foot through, woods where the wood thrush forever sings, where the hours are early morning ones, and there is dew on the grass, and the day is forever unproved, where I might have a fertile unknown for a soil about me.

❦

I HAD two friends. The one offered me friendship on such terms that I could not accept it, without a sense of degradation. He would not meet me on equal terms, but only be to some extent my patron. He would not come to see, but was hurt if I did not visit him. He would not readily accept a favor, but would gladly confer one. He treated me with ceremony occasionally, though he could be simple and downright sometimes; and from time to time acted a part, treating me as if I were a distinguished stranger; was on stilts, using made words. Our relation was one long tragedy, yet I did not directly speak of it. I do not believe in complaint, nor in explanation. The whole is but too plain, alas, already. We grieve that we do not love each other, that we cannot confide in each other. I could not bring myself to speak, and so recognize an obstacle to our affection.

I had another friend, who, through a slight obtuseness, perchance, did not recognize a fact which the dignity of friendship would by no means allow me to descend so far as to speak of, and yet the inevitable effect of that ignorance was to hold us apart forever.

❧

The first of the 'two friends' Thoreau speaks of was Emerson. The following excerpts from three letters of 1843 tell a related story. There is an undercurrent in them which brings to mind Wilder's comment, 'Whenever I think of Thoreau, I feel a weight about my heart'; yet, their first theme is joy, of a kind peculiar to those who see beyond the framework of mortal affairs. It is joy suggestive of an innocence not commonly celebrated in modern relationships.

FROM A LETTER TO EMERSON

I have made slight acquaintance also with one Mrs. Lidian Emerson, who almost persuades me to be a Christian, but I fear I as often lapse into Heathenism.

❧

FROM TWO LETTERS TO MRS. R. W. EMERSON
My dear Friend, —

I believe a good many conversations with you were left in an unfinished state, and now indeed I don't know where to take them up. But I will resume some of the unfinished silence. I shall not hesitate to know you. I think of you as some elder sister of mine, whom I could not have avoided,— a sort of lunar influence,—only of such age as the moon, whose time is measured by her light. You must know that you represent to me woman, for I have not traveled very far or wide,—and what if I had?

YOU HAVE HELPED to keep my life 'on loft,' as Chaucer says of Griselda, and in a better sense. You always seemed to look down at me as from some elevation—some of your high humilities—and I was better for having to look up. I felt taxed not to disappoint your expectation; for could there be any accident so sad as to be respected for something better than we are?

∗

MY VERY DEAR FRIEND,

I have only read a page of your letter and have come out to the top of the hill at sunset where I can see the ocean to prepare to read the rest. It is fitter that it should hear it than the walls of my chamber. The very crickets here seem to chirp around me as they did not before. I feel as if it were a great daring to go on and read the rest, and then to live accordingly. There are more than thirty vessels in sight going to sea. I am almost afraid to look at your letter. I see that it will make my life very steep, but it may lead to fairer prospects than this.

Friendship and Singularity

You seem to me to speak out of a very clear and high heaven, where any one may be who stands so high. Your voice seems not a voice, but comes as much from the blue heavens, as from the paper.

My dear friend it was very noble in you to write me so trustful an answer. It will do as well for another world as for this. Such a voice is for no particular time nor person, and it makes him who may hear it stand for all that is lofty and true in humanity. The thought of you will constantly elevate my life; it will be something always above the horizon to behold, as when I look up at the evening star. I think I know your thoughts without seeing you, and as well here as in Concord. You are not at all strange to me.

I, PERHAPS, am more willing to deceive by appearances than you say you are; it would not be worth the while to tell how willing — but I have the power perhaps too much to forget my meanness as soon as seen, and not be incited by permanent sorrow.

WHAT WEALTH IS IT to have such friends that we cannot think of them without elevation. And we can think of them any time, and any where, and it costs nothing but the lofty disposition. I cannot tell you the joy your letter gives me — which will not quite cease till the latest time. Let me accompany your finest thought.

I send my love to my other friend and brother, whose nobleness I slowly recognize.

❧

The story taken up in the preceding letters passed on to a sober conclusion. Lidian Emerson's response to Thoreau's sentiments is lost, but his next extant correspondence with the Emerson household leaves the distinct impression that her reply was guarded, at best. In the extraordinary, brief passage quoted here, and in three subsequent Journal *entries of much later years, one senses the degree of Thoreau's ambivalence toward humankind. It is, however, an ambivalence tempered by a thoughtful nature . . . and, here and there, by a welcome and almost mischievous sense of humor.*

FROM A LETTER
TO MR. AND MRS. R. W. EMERSON

But know, my friends, that I a good deal hate you all in my most private thoughts—as the substratum of the little love I bear you. Though you are a rare band and do not make half use enough of one another.

❧

I ASSOCIATE the idea of friendship, methinks, with the person the most foreign to me. This illusion is perpetuated, like superstition in a country long after civilization has been attained to. We are attracted toward a particular person, but no one has discovered the laws of this attraction. When I come nearest to that other actually, I am wont to be surprised at my selection. It may be enough that we have met some time, and now can never forget it. Some time or other we paid each other this wonderful compliment, looked largely, humanly, divinely on one another, and now are fated to be acquaintances forever. In the case of nature I am not so conscious of this unsatisfied yearning.

※

WHAT IF WE FEEL a yearning to which no breast answers? I walk alone. My heart is full. Feelings impede the current of my thoughts. I knock on the earth for my friend. I expect to meet him at every turn; but no friend appears, and perhaps none is dreaming of me. I am tired of frivolous society, in which silence is forever the most natural and the best manners. I would fain walk on the deep waters, but my companions will only walk on shallows and puddles. I am naturally silent in the midst of twenty from day to day, from year to year. I am rarely reminded of their presence. Two yards of politeness do not make society for me. One complains that I do not take his jokes. I took them before he had done uttering them, and went my way. One talks to me of his apples and pears, and I depart with my secret untold.

※

THE OBSTACLES which the heart meets with are like granite blocks which one alone cannot move. She who was as the morning light to me is now neither the morning star nor the evening star. We meet but to find each other further asunder, and the oftener we meet the more rapid our divergence. So a star of the first magnitude pales in the heavens, not from any fault in the observer's eye nor from any fault in itself, perchance, but because its progress in its own system has put a greater distance between.

The night is oracular. What have been the intimations of the night? I ask How have you passed the night? Goodnight!

My friend will be bold to conjecture; he will guess bravely at the significance of my words.

WINTER, with its *inwardness*, is upon us. A man is constrained to sit down, and to think.

JOHN BROWN

It is doubtful that any other man he met so struck Thoreau as did John Brown. One may accept the psychoanalytic view that an identification with Brown fulfilled a critical need in Thoreau to align himself with active and rebellious forces; or, one may simply take his words at their poetic, practical and philosophical face values. The net impact is the same. Brown stood for *something, and the size of what he symbolized is, perhaps, too much for us to fully grasp.*

JOHN BROWN'S career for the last six weeks of his life was meteor-like, flashing through the darkness in which we live. I know of nothing so miraculous in our history.

FOR MY OWN PART, I commonly attend more to nature than to man, but any affecting human event may blind our eyes to natural objects. I was so absorbed in him as to be surprised whenever I detected the routine of the natural world surviving still, or met persons going about their affairs indifferent. It appeared strange to me that the 'little dipper' should be still diving quietly in the river, as of yore; and it suggested that this bird might continue to dive here when Concord should be no more.

I felt that he, a prisoner in the midst of his enemies and under sentence of death, if consulted as to his next step or resource would answer more wisely than all his country-men beside. He best understood his position; he contem-plated it most calmly. Comparatively, all other men, North and South, were beside themselves. Our thought could not revert to any greater or wiser or better man with whom to contrast him, for he, then and there, was above them all. The man this country was about to hang appeared the greatest and best in it.

Years were not required for a revolution of public opinion; days, nay hours, produced marked changes in this case. Fifty who were ready to say, on going into our meeting in honor of him in Concord, that he ought to be hung, would not say it when they came out. They heard his words read; they saw the earnest faces of the congregation; and perhaps they joined at last in singing the hymn in his praise.

THEY, whether within the Church or out of it, who adhere to the spirit and let go the letter, and are accordingly called infidel, were as usual foremost to recognize him. Men have been hung in the South before for attempting to rescue slaves, and the North was not much stirred by it. Whence, then, this wonderful difference? We were not so sure of their devotion to principle. We made a subtle distinction, forgot human laws, and did homage to an idea. The North, I mean the living North, was suddenly all transcendental. It went behind the human law, it went behind the apparent failure, and recognized eternal justice and glory. Commonly, men live according to a formula, and are satisfied if the order of law is observed, but in this instance they, to some extent, returned to original perceptions, and there was a slight revival of old religion. They saw that what was called order was confusion, what was called justice, injustice, and that the best was deemed the worst.

WHEN A NOBLE DEED is done, who is likely to appreciate it? They who are noble themselves. I was not surprised that certain of my neighbors spoke of John Brown as an ordinary felon, for who are they? They have either much flesh, or much office, or much coarseness of some kind. They are not ethereal natures in any sense. The dark qualities predominate in them. Several of them are decidedly pachydermatous. I say it in sorrow, not in anger. How can a man behold the light who has no answering inward light? They are true to their sight, but when they look this way they see nothing, they are blind. For the children of the light to contend with them is as if there should be a contest between eagles and owls. Show me a man who feels bitterly toward John Brown, and let me hear what noble verse he can repeat. He'll be as dumb as if his lips were stone.

It is not every man who can be a Christian, even in a very moderate sense, whatever education you give him. It is a matter of constitution and temperament, after all. He may have to be born again many times. I have known many a man who pretended to be a Christian, in whom it was ridiculous, for he had no genius for it. It is not every man who can be a free man, even.

Editors persevered for a good while in saying that Brown was crazy; but at last they said only that it was 'a crazy scheme,' and the only evidence brought to prove it was that it cost him his life. I have no doubt that if he had gone with five thousand men, liberated a thousand slaves, killed a hundred or two slaveholders, and had as many more killed on his own side, but not lost his own life, these same editors would have called it by a more respectable name. Yet he has been far more successful than that. He has liberated many thousands of slaves, both North and South. They seem to have known nothing about living or dying for a principle. They all called him crazy then; who calls him crazy now?

LITERARY GENTLEMEN, editors, and critics think that they know how to write, because they have studied grammar and rhetoric; but they are egregiously mistaken. The art of composition is as simple as the discharge of a bullet from a rifle, and its masterpieces imply an infinitely greater force behind them. This unlettered man's speaking and writing are standard English. Some words and phrases deemed vulgarisms and Americanisms before, he has made standard American; such as 'It will pay.' It suggests that the one great rule of composition—and if I were a professor of rhetoric I should insist on this—is, to speak the truth. This first, this second, this third; pebbles in your mouth or not. This demands earnestness and manhood chiefly.

NOTHING could his enemies do but it redounded to his infinite advantage,—that is, to the advantage of his cause. They did not hang him at once, but reserved him to preach to them. And then there was another great blunder. They did not hang his four followers with him; that scene was still postponed; and so his victory was prolonged and completed. No theatrical manager could have arranged things so wisely to give effect to his behavior and words. And who, think you, was the manager? Who placed the slave-woman and her child, whom he stooped to kiss for a symbol, between his prison and the gallows?

ON THE DAY of his translation, I heard, to be sure, that he was hung, but I did not know what that meant; I felt no sorrow on that account; but not for a day or two did I even hear that he was dead, and not after any number of days shall I believe it. Of all the men who were said to be my contemporaries, it seemed to me that John Brown was the only one who had not died. I never hear of a man named Brown now,—and I hear of them pretty often,—I never hear of any particularly brave and earnest man, but my first thought is of John Brown, and what relation he may be to him. I meet him at every turn. He is more alive than ever he was. He has earned immortality. He is not confined to North Elba nor to Kansas. He is no longer working in secret. He works in public, and in the clearest light that shines on this land.

LATE THOUGHTS

✢

On the cover of the original theatre program for Clear Sky, Pure Light *is a piece of photographic serendipity: the sun, emerging from a trailing edge of cloud, its rays refracted in a chance, striking pattern by the camera lens. No contrived effect could more symbolically have suggested the intention of the play . . . or the character of the man whom it portrayed.*

Nearly a century and a quarter earlier, on the same Concord hillside where that photograph was taken, Thoreau had found occasion to remark on the unique, evocative power of the light.

As I sat at the wall-corner, high on Conantum, the sky generally covered with continuous cheerless-looking slate-colored clouds, except in the west, I saw, through the hollows of the clouds, here and there the blue appearing. All at once a low-slanted glade of sunlight from one of heaven's west windows behind me fell on the bare gray maples, lighting them up with an incredibly intense and pure white light; then, going out there, it lit up some white birch stems south of the pond, then the gray rocks and the pale reddish young oaks of the lower cliffs, and then the very pale brown meadow-grass, and at last the brilliant white breasts of two ducks, tossing on the agitated surface far off on the pond, which I had not detected before. It was but a transient ray, and there was no sunshine afterward, but the intensity of the light was surprising and impressive, like a halo, a glory in which only the just deserved to live.

It was as if the air, purified by the long storm, reflected these few rays from side to side with a complete illumination, like a perfectly polished mirror, while the effect was greatly enhanced by the contrast with the dull dark clouds and sombre earth. As if Nature did not dare at once to let in the full blaze of the sun to this combustible atmosphere. It was a serene, elysian light, in which the deeds I have dreamed of but not realized might have been performed. At the eleventh hour, late in the year, we have visions of the life we might have lived. No perfectly fair weather ever offered such an arena for noble acts. It was such a light as we behold but dwell not in! In each case, every recess was filled and lit up with this pure white light. The maples were Potter's, far down stream, but I dreamed I walked like a liberated spirit in their maze. The withered meadow-grass was as soft and glorious as paradise. And then it was remarkable that the light-giver should have revealed to me, for all life, the heaving white breasts of those two ducks within this glade of light. It was extinguished and relit as it travelled.

Tell me precisely the value and significance of these transient gleams which come sometimes at the end of the day, before the close of the storm, final dispersion of the clouds, too late to be of any service to the works of man for the day, and notwithstanding the whole night after may be overcast! Is not this a language to be heard and understood? There is, in the brown and gray earth and rocks, and the withered leaves and bare twigs at this season, a purity more correspondent to the light itself than summer offers.

DEPARTURE

❧

The story is told that in his last moment, Thomas Edison sat bolt upright in bed and, staring straight ahead, exclaimed, 'I am surprised! It is very beautiful over there.' It seems likely that what surprised Edison appeared self-evident to Thoreau, who might well have countered that, to the perceptive soul, it was often equally beautiful over here.

There is something satisfying in the thought that great men make some of their most intriguing statements as their lives draw to a close.

THE WINTER is coming when I shall walk the sky.

❧

WHEN I WAS a very little boy I learned that I must die, and I set that down, so of course I am not disappointed now. Death is as near to you as it is to me.

❧

BUT THERE IS an aftermath in early autumn, and some spring flowers bloom again, followed by an Indian summer of finer atmosphere and of a pensive beauty. May my life be not destitute of its Indian summer, a season of fine and clear, mild weather in which I may prolong my hunting before the winter comes, when I may once more lie on the ground with faith, as in spring, and even with more serene confidence. And then I will [wrap the] drapery of summer about me and lie down to pleasant dreams. As one year passes into another through the medium of winter, so does this our life pass into another through the medium of death.

❧

BUT HARK! I hear the tolling of a distant funeral bell, and

[93]

they are conveying a corpse to the churchyard from one of the houses that I see, and its serious sound is more in harmony with this scenery than any ordinary bustle could be. It suggests that a man must die to his present life before he can appreciate his opportunities and the beauty of the abode that is appointed him.

❦

WHATEVER ACTUALLY HAPPENS to a man is wonderfully trivial and insignificant,—even to death itself, I imagine.

THIS STREAM OF EVENTS which we consent to call actual, and that other mightier stream which alone carries us with it,—what makes the difference? On the one our bodies float, and we have sympathy with it through them; on the other, our spirits. We are ever dying to one world and being born into another, and possibly no man knows whether he is at any time dead in the sense in which he affirms that phenomenon of another, or not.

❦

ONE WORLD at a time.

❦

I SHALL LEAVE the world without regret.

❦

IT IS BETTER some things should end.

Departure

❧

In the last days of his life, Thoreau was asked by his Aunt Louisa whether he had 'made his peace with God.' In what must qualify as one of the most gentle, eloquent, and terminal rejoinders ever given, he responded with a sentence which sums up, precisely, the true thrust of his accomplishments:

I DID NOT KNOW we had ever quarrelled, Aunt.

Appendix: Sources

❧

*Source references within brackets are made
to the following texts*

Thoreau's *Journal* [*J*]
A Week on the Concord and Merrimack Rivers [*Wk*]
    page references to the Apollo paperback edition of 1966
Walden [*Wal*]
    page references to the W.W. Norton edition of 1951,
    reprinted by Bramhall House, New York
The Correspondence of Henry David Thoreau [*Corr*]
    ed. by Walter Harding and Carl Bode; New York
    University Press, 1958
The Days of Henry Thoreau [*Days of H T*]
    Harding; Alfred A. Knopf, New York, 1966
'Civil Disobedience' [*Civ Dis*]
'The Last Days of John Brown' [*Last Days*]

Several of these editions are out of print, but may be found in libraries or at such organizations as the Thoreau Lyceum in Concord.

A number of the selections in this volume may also be found in *Thoreau's World: Miniatures From His Journal*, ed. by Charles R. Anderson, Prentice-Hall 1971 (currently out of print, but available as indicated above), and in *A Thoreau Profile*, by Walter Harding and Milton Meltzer, a Thoreau Foundation paperback available through the Thoreau Lyceum, 156 Belknap St., Concord, Mass. 01742.

The two comments by Thornton Wilder which are quoted in the section, 'Friendship and Singularity,' are excerpted from the essay, 'The American Loneliness,' which appeared in the *Atlantic Monthly* of August, 1952. They are reprinted here through the courtesy of the firm of Brandt and Brandt.

––––––––––

A Preface: Speech and Silence

As the truest society . . . [*Wk*, Friday, pp. 489–491]
Do not speak for other men . . . [*J*, III, pp. 157–158, 25 Dec. 1851]

River: Wildness and Civilization

Quoted in commentary: 'we two . . .' [*Wk*, Saturday, p. 11]
I have never got over my surprise . . . [*J*, IX, p. 160, 5 Dec. 1856]

I think I could write a poem . . . [*J*, I, p. 282, 4 Sept. 1841]
Concord River is remarkable . . . [*Wk*, Concord River, p. 6]
With such thoughts . . . [*Wk*, Saturday, p. 15]
Gradually the village murmur . . . [*Wk*, Saturday, p. 17]
By noon we were let down . . . [*Wk*, Sunday, p. 92]
We were thus entering the State . . . [*Wk*, Sunday, pp. 98–103]
Some spring the white man came . . . [*Wk*, Sunday, pp. 58–59]
We talk of civilizing the Indian . . . [*Wk*, Sunday, pp. 62–63]
I am convinced that my genius . . . [*Wk*, Sunday, pp. 60–61]
Heal yourselves, doctors . . . [*Wk*, Monday, p. 213]

Gods
Entire Selection [*Wk*, Sunday, pp. 75–82]

On Being a Writer
Entire Selection [*J*, V, pp. 459–460, 28 Oct. 1853]

Loss
Quoted in commentary: 'drive life into a corner' and
  'whether it is of the devil or of God' [*Wal*, Where I
  Lived and What I Lived For, p. 106]
The sun has just burst through . . . [letter to Emerson, 11
  March 1842; *Corr* pp. 63–65]
Only nature has a right to grieve . . . [letter to Mrs. Lucy
  Brown, 2 March 1842; *Corr* pp. 62–63]

On Improvements
Entire Selection [*Wal*, Economy, pp. 18–22]

Clear Sky, Pure Light

The Woods, and Walden
For a long time I was reporter… [*Wal*, Economy, pp. 32–36]
Nevertheless, of all the characters . . . [*Wal*, The Ponds, pp. 212–213]

Resistance to Civil Government
Entire Selection [*Civ Dis*]

Return
When I wrote the following pages… [*Wal*, Economy, p.17]
But Why I changed? why I left . . . [*J*, III, pp. 214–215, 22 Jan. 1852]
I left the woods for as good a reason . . . [*Wal*, Conclusion, p. 343]
I must say that I do not know . . . [*J*, III, p. 216, 22 Jan. 1852]
I learned this, at least . . . [*Wal*, Conclusion, pp. 343–345]

On the Nature and Origin of an Accident
Entire Selection [*J*, II, pp. 21–25, 1850]

Friendship and Singularity
I know of but one or two persons . . . [*J*, XI, pp. 296–297, 8 Nov. 1858]
We have such a habit of looking away . . . [*J*, XIII, pp. 141–142, 12 Feb. 1860 (paragraph order inverted)]

Everywhere snow, gathered . . . [*J*, III, pp. 312–313, 18 Feb. 1852]

I knew a crazy man . . . [*J*, VI, p. 86, 30 Jan. 1854]

Here I am at home . . . [*J*, XI, p. 275, 1 Nov. 1858]

How long we will follow an illusion! . . . [*J*, XI, pp. 281–282, 3 Nov. 1858]

I long for wildness . . . [*J*, V, p. 293, 22 June 1853]

I had two friends . . . [*J*, VIII, p. 199, 4 March 1856]

I have made slight acquaintance . . . [letter to Emerson, 24 Jan. 1843; *Corr* pp. 76–78]

My dear Friend,—I believe . . . [letter to Mrs. R.W. Emerson, 22 May 1843; *Corr* pp. 103–104]

My very dear Friend, I have only . . . [letter to Mrs. R.W. Emerson, 20 June 1843; *Corr* pp. 119–120]

But know, my friends . . . [letter to Mr. and Mrs. R.W. Emerson, 8 July 1843; *Corr* pp. 123–125]

I associate the idea of friendship . . . [*J*, XI, p. 282, 3 Nov. 1858]

What if we feel a yearning . . . [*J*, VII, pp. 416–417, 11 June 1855]

The obstacles which the heart meets . . . [*J*, III, pp. 82–83, 27 October 1851]

John Brown
Entire Selection [*Last Days*]

Clear Sky, Pure Light

Late Thoughts
Entire Selection [*J*, X, pp. 132–134, 28 Oct. 1857]

Departure
The winter is coming . . . [*J*, XIII, p. 142, 12 Feb. 1860]
When I was a very little boy . . . [*Days of H T*, p. 464]
But there is an aftermath . . . .[*J*, II, pp. 481–482, 8 Sept. 1851]
But hark! I hear the tolling . . . [*J*, X, pp. 73–74, 7 Oct. 1857]
Whatever actually happens to a man . . . [*J*, II, p. 43, bet. 16 July–31 Aug. 1850]
One world at a time . . . [*Days of H T*, p. 465]
I shall leave the world without regret . . . [*Days of H T*, p. 462]
It is better some things should end . . . [*Days of H T*, p. 462]
I did not know we had ever quarreled . . . [*Days of H T*, p. 464]

Unless otherwise indicated,

spelling and punctuation in all selections

are as in the original.

2000 COPIES

❧

Designed & set in Monotype Van Dijck
and printed letterpress by
Michael and Winifred Bixler

for
THE PENMAEN PRESS